DATE DUE

MAKE IT POP!

Activities and Adventures in POP ART

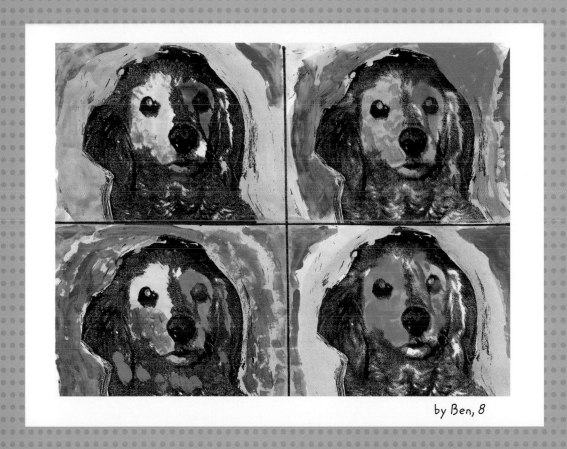

by Ben, 8

JOYCE RAIMONDO

Watson-Guptill Publications/New York

For my nephew, Raymond Raimondo, and my nieces Christa, Jacqueline, Brittany, and Suzanne Clay, with love.

by Ms. Reboli's art class

Copyright © 2006 by Joyce Raimondo

First published in 2006 by Watson-Guptill Publications
Crown Publishing Group, a division of Random House Inc., New York
www.crownpublishing.com
www.watsonguptill.com

Step-by-step artwork by Joyce Raimondo. Photographs of three-dimensional art by Frank Roccanova.

Photo credits: Page 9, *Marilyn Diptych* by Andy Warhol, 1962. Synthetic polymer paint and silkscreen ink on canvas, 6'10" x 57" (205.4 x 144.8 cm). Copyright © 2006 The Andy Warhol Foundation for the Visual Arts / ARS, NY. Tate Gallery, London / Art Resource, NY. Tate Gallery, London, Great Britain. TM 2006 Marilyn Monroe LLC licensed by CMG Worldwide Inc., USA. www.MarilynMonroe.com. Cover and page 17, *Girl with Ball* by Roy Lichtenstein. © Estate of Roy Lichtenstein. Page 23, *Map* by Jasper Johns. Art copyright © Jasper Johns / Licensed by VAGA, New York, NY. Digital image © The Museum of Modern Art / Licensed by SCALA / Art Resource, NY. Jasper Johns (b. 1930) © VAGA, NY. *Map.* 1961. Oil on canvas, 6'6" x 10' 3 1/8". Gift of Mr. and Mrs. Robert C. Scull. (277.1963) The Museum of Modern Art, New York, NY, U.S.A. Page 29, *Retroactive I* by Robert Rauschenberg. Art copyright © Robert Rauschenberg / Licensed by VAGA, New York, NY. Wadsworth Atheneum Museum of Art, Hartford, CT. Gift of Susan Morse Hilles. Page 35, *Soft Fur Good Humors* by Claes Oldenburg, 1963. Fake fur filled with kapok and wood painted with enamel. Four, each 2 x 9 1/2 x 19 inches (5.1 x 24.1 x 48.3 cm). Private collection, United States. Copyright © Claes Oldenburg. Page 43, *Diner* by George Segal. Art copyright © The George and Helen Segal Foundation / Licensed by VAGA, New York, NY. Collection Walker Art Center, Minneapolis. Gift of the T.B. Walker Foundation, 1966.

Every effort has been made to ensure accuracy in this book and to acknowledge all copyright holders. We will be pleased to correct any inadvertent errors or omissions in future editions.

Library of Congress Cataloging-in-Publication Data

Raimondo, Joyce.
  Make it pop! : activities and adventures in Pop art / Joyce Raimondo.
      p. cm. — (Art explorers)
  Includes bibliographical references and index.
  ISBN 0-8230-2507-1 (alk. paper)
  1. Pop art—United States—Juvenile literature. 2. Art—Study and teaching
(Primary)—Activity programs. I. Title. II. Series: Raimondo, Joyce. Art explorers.
  N6512.5.P6R35 2006
  709.04'071—dc22

                                    2006012957

Senior Acquisitions Editor: Julie Mazur
Project Editor: Laaren Brown
Designer: Edward Miller
Production Manager: Ellen Greene
The typefaces in this book include Futura, Typography of Coop, and Ad Lib.

Manufactured in Singapore

First printing, 2006

3 4 5 6 7 / 12 11 10

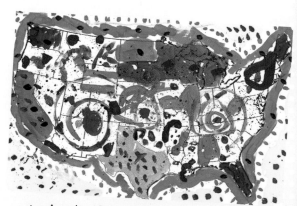

by Angela, 10

by Raja, 11

by Project
Most kids

Contents

by Sheryl, 7

by Brian, 10

Help Your Child Explore Pop Art

by Janet Alexandra, and Allison, 11

Make It Pop! invites children to **explore Pop Art** and use it as a springboard for their own creativity. The discussions in this book encourage children to **examine works of art** and **develop their own personal interpretations**. Related projects encourage children to create their own art inspired by Pop artists' ideas and techniques.

What do you see in this picture?

Pop artists transformed **popular culture** into thought-provoking works of art. Children immediately relate to the subjects in these works—celebrities, brand names, media images, comics, fast food, and consumer goods—that are taken from contemporary life. The questions in this book **motivate creative thinking** by asking children to describe and interpret what they see. Let go of your own ideas, and affirm the children's insights. In a group, **encourage different opinions**. Older children may want to research the artists' lives, and they can start with the biographies in this book.

Create your own Pop Art

Make It Pop! invites children to become aware of pop culture and use it creatively for art. Some Pop artists copied images from the media using mechanical printing processes. Others imitated the glossy look of mass-produced pictures with flat bright colors and bold outlines. Pop sculptors incorporated actual consumer goods into their artworks or created whimsical monuments based on popular everyday items. The projects in this book encourage kids to explore the ideas and methods of famous Pop artists with materials adapted for children.

Look around!

Begin your exploration of Pop Art with a lively conversation. Collect brand-name products, candy wrappers, fast-food containers, and advertisements, and use them as a basis for discussion. For example, ask children to identify popular logos such as McDonald's golden arches or Nike's swoosh.

by Joe, 9

Talk about what an advertisement is selling and how it persuades us to buy something. Avoid judgments. **Discuss the famous pictures** in this book to **spark ideas**.

Everyone is creative

The art instructions guide young artists on **a journey of discovery**. Do not expect children to follow them exactly. Demonstrate techniques—such as how to make a print or use papier-mâché. Then let kids work with a spirit of experimentation. Everyone has his or her own **way of making art**, and **creativity is a gift to be nurtured in everyone**.

by Allison M., 9

by Michelle, 8

Pop Art

This book highlights six American Pop artists who created a new art that shocked the art world. Emerging in the mid-1950s and 60s, young artists used images taken directly from popular culture—advertising, mass media, consumer goods, brand names, and film, television, and celebrity icons—and turned them into sophisticated artworks. Rejecting Abstract Expressionism, which showed the artist's inner life in abstract paintings, Pop artists pictured recognizable subjects from the contemporary consumer world around them.

Working in New York City in the 1950s, Jasper Johns and Robert Rauschenberg blurred the boundary between art and everyday life. Transient images and products that are constantly bought, sold, and thrown away—these are the materials of Rauschenberg's stunning works. He collected discarded objects and newspaper photographs and combined them with paint or silk screening on huge colorful canvases. Painting "things the mind already knows," Johns pictured familiar objects such as flags, maps, and targets, and sometimes attached actual objects to his paintings.

During the 1960s, Andy Warhol and Roy Lichtenstein created colorful images found in mass media and adapted the procedures of modern printing. Eliminating the hand of the individual artist, Warhol and his assistants copied news photographs, brand names, and Hollywood stars, repeating their images with photographic silk screening. Lichtenstein imitated the look of mechanical reproduction, painting giant comics with bold outlines, flat bright colors, and Benday dots.

Inspired by urban life, George Segal placed plaster figures in real settings to capture daily routines of contemporary America. Claes Oldenburg turned ordinary objects into huge monuments on city streets, transformed them into soft sculptures, and made plaster versions of consumer goods and fast food.

Pop artists challenge us to see our world in a new way. Like a mirror, their images invite us to look, to question, and to celebrate the popular culture of today.

Make It Pop!

by Maggie, 10

This book invites you to **explore the fun-filled world of Pop Art**. The word "Pop" is short for popular. Pop Artists **turn popular things and people into great works of art**. Look at the pictures in this book, and talk about what you see. Then create your own Pop Art.

What's popular **today**? What **soda** is so popular that people drink it all over the world? Which **fast-food** restaurant is so famous that you can find one almost anywhere? What popular **brand-name products** do you buy? Can you think of a **famous person** who is so popular, everyone knows his or her name?

Think about it. How does something become popular? Today, we see celebrities and brand-name things over and over again in **movies, TV shows, magazines, newspapers,** and **advertisements**. Soon we know their names. Would you want to be famous? What would you be known for?

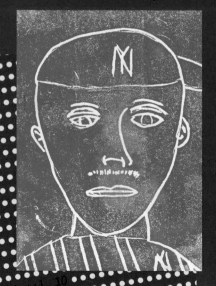

by Matthew L., 10

by Kenneth, 10

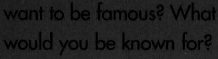

Wacky Colors

by Ms. Reboli's art class

Wackey Colors

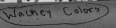

8

Discover how Pop artists turn **popular people** into imaginative artworks. You will find a movie star with pink skin and a pretty girl who is a gigantic cartoon! Try it yourself! Print out a colorful famous face, paint a huge cartoon, or make yourself the star of your art.

Find out how Pop artists change **everyday things** into amazing works of art. Imagine an ice-cream pop that is as long as your arm or a mixed-up map that is filled with swirling paint! Sculpt a giant candy bar, make fake fast food out of clay, or paint a poster of your favorite sneakers.

Learn how Pop artists use **throwaway stuff**— magazines, toys, stuffed animals, and things they find— to make a masterpiece. You can, too! Don't throw away your old **junk**. Collect it, and **recycle** it for art!

Look around—**what do you see**? Turn your favorite people and things into Pop Art. And remember—your art can be as **silly** or **colorful** or **strange** as you want it to be.

WHAT'S POPULAR?

ANDY WARHOL

Picture a movie star with a pink face and bright yellow hair! That's what the artist Andy Warhol did when he made this portrait of the famous actress Marilyn Monroe. Warhol clipped a photograph of the beautiful movie star from a newspaper. Instead of painting her picture by hand with a paintbrush, Warhol and his helpers printed out her photo with ink using a special way of making art called photo-silkscreening. As you can see, instead of using normal skin colors, he printed the popular star's face over and over again in fun colors and black and white.

Warhol was fascinated with the way people and products become so popular that everyone knows them. Mickey Mouse, Elvis Presley, Coca-Cola, Campbell's Soup! Do you know their names? Warhol printed thousands of colorful pictures of famous movie actors, singers, brand-name foods, and cartoon characters. Many people loved his Pop Art prints, and Warhol became a rich and famous art star!

Can you think of a person who is so famous that everyone knows who he or she is? Who is your favorite actress, athlete, singer, or comedian?

- Do you **recognize** this **famous person**? Do you know what she became famous for?
- How many faces do you see here? How is each one **different**? What is **similar** about them?
- How would you **describe these faces**? Do they look **beautiful, scary,** or **funny**? What makes you say that? What other words would you use to describe them?
- What is **unusual** about her faces? What looks **make-believe**? What looks **real**?
- Look at her **expression**. How do you think she **feels**?

- Look closely. What do you notice about the **lips** and **eyes**?
- Warhol found a **photograph** of this face and **printed it** in his artwork. How do you think he **changed** the photograph to create this artwork?
- Think about most artworks of people that you have seen. How is this one different?

Marilyn Diptych, 1962
synthetic polymer paint and silkscreen ink on canvas
57 x 82 inches
Tate Gallery, London, England

How does a person become famous? Where do you see a celebrity's face again and again and again?

Print it out! Color it in!
This section invites you to change popular people and products into colorful works of art.

9

Celebrity Portraits

Make colorful portraits of a famous person using Styrofoam printing.

Movie stars, singers, baseball players . . . a person becomes famous when you see his or her photograph on television or in movies, newspapers, or magazines. Can you think of someone who is so popular today, you see his or her face just about everywhere? Like Warhol, picture a famous face. Print it again and again in wild colors.

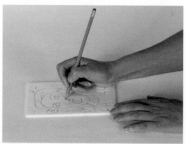

1. Choose a famous person—an athlete, movie star, singer, comedian, or the president. You can collect photographs from magazines or the internet to remind you what the person looks like.

2. Make a printing plate out of Styrofoam. You can buy Styrofoam sheets from an art-supply store, or cut a rectangle out of a disposable Styrofoam dish or clean meat-packing tray.

3. Press lines into the Styrofoam with a pencil to draw the face. Notice how the lines are actually carved into the sheet. (If you press too lightly, your picture will not show up. Draw large, simple shapes and lines. Details that are too tiny will not work.) Write any words and letters backward.

4. Add details to tell about the person. I made the comedian Jim Carrey. I wrote "Ha-ha" for laughter. You can add a baseball bat and cap for a ballplayer or a microphone for a singer.

5. Roll ink onto the Styrofoam with a brayer (roller). Try to get an even coat. Do not put too much ink on your brayer; it will fill up the lines. Notice how the lines show up white!

6. Place a sheet of paper over the Styrofoam. Gently rub and press with your hand or a clean brayer.

7. Surprise! Lift up the paper to see your print.

8. Copy it, and change the colors! Wash your Styrofoam plate and dry it completely. Roll on a new color, and print another face. Or you can use more than one color ink on your plate at a time. Try printing on different colored papers. Then, like Warhol, arrange all your copies to make one colorful artwork.

My favorite comedian, Jim Carrey

Supplies

Water-based printing ink (or tempera paint)
Brayer (roller)

Paper
Pencil
Styrofoam sheet

Harry Potter.—Matthew P., 10

Gary Sheffield.—Matthew L., 10

Paris Hilton.—Evelyn, 10

Try these, too!

Colorful Collage Prints

Warhol became well known, and many famous people hired him to make their portraits. Sometimes he printed their faces on top of a collage to create playful pictures. Try it yourself: Cut and paste simple paper shapes flat on a paper. Let dry, then print a face over it.

Play Money

In one of his artworks, Warhol made pictures of dollar bills, showing George Washington's face. Everyone can recognize the first American president because he is on every U.S. dollar. Draw a picture of a dollar bill—but put a new face in the middle. Whose face would you like to show? Martin Luther King's, Michael Jordan's, maybe your own?

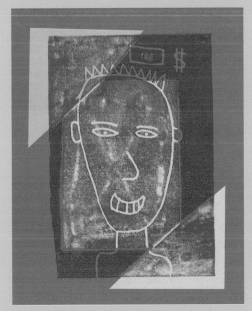

I'm rich and famous!
—Scotty, 9

Mary-Kate and Ashley.—Bridget, 9

Copy Me!

More Warhol art

Make a group of fun portraits using photocopies and paint.
Warhol printed hundreds of colorful pictures of Marilyn Monroe. In some of them, he mixed up all the colors. Picture a face that's green, pink, yellow, or bright blue! Warhol changed the colors of her eyes and hair, too. Make yourself a colorful star! Photocopy your face and paint the copies funny colors. (You can also copy the face of a friend, a famous person, or your pet.)

1. Take a photograph of your face, or find one. If you do not have a photograph, draw a picture of your face.

2. Enlarge it! Ask an adult to help. Go to a printing store or a photocopy machine. Make an enlarged black-and-white copy of your face that fills an $8\frac{1}{2}$ x 11-inch paper.

3. Copy it. Make many photocopies of the picture. (Print it onto a heavy paper. Make it high contrast so it will be easier to paint.) If you cannot get to a photocopy machine, just make a few drawings of your face.

4. Paint your face and hair funny colors. I made my faces yellow, orange, pink, and blue! It is also fun to paint colorful teeth, lips, and eyes. Paint in your clothes. (Remember, wash your paintbrush before you use a new color to keep the colors bright.)

5. Paint the background. You can add fun designs, if you like, such as dots or stripes.

6. Colorful you! Display all your pictures together for your artwork.

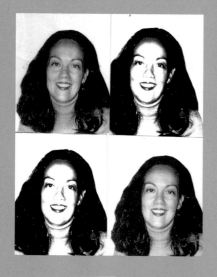 ▶ 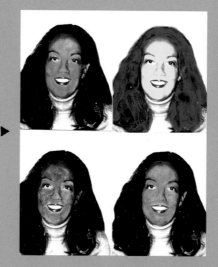 ▶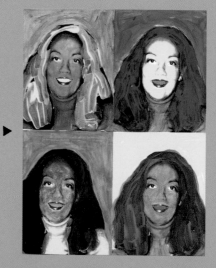

Supplies

Photograph or drawing of your face
Photocopies
Painting supplies

In the future, everyone will be world-famous for fifteen minutes.
—Andy Warhol

Colorful imagination.
—Hannah and Jasmine, 8

Laughing out loud.—Peter, 8

Try this, too!

In the News

Warhol loved to clip photographs from newspapers for his art. He even collected photos of bad news such as airplane crashes. Create your own newspaper artwork. Write the name of the paper and a headline for a news story. Cut and paste a photograph from a newspaper or draw a picture of your news story. You can show a famous person or an exciting sports event, or even put yourself in the paper. Make photocopies and paint them. Arrange your copies in a giant artwork, or give your newspaper to friends.

Cool news.—Joseph, 8

Favorite Brand Names

Another Warhol idea

Paint a popular brand-name food using watercolors and marker.
Cheerios! Hershey's Kisses! Have you heard of these? How does a food become so popular? The special name, fancy letters, and fun package, plus advertising, make sure everyone will remember a brand-name food. Warhol often pictured popular products such as Coca-Cola and Campbell's Soup in his art.

1. What famous foods do you eat? Look around the supermarket or in your kitchen. Do you have a favorite candy, cereal, soda, or ice cream? Choose a food for your artwork. Look at the package. What makes it special? Does it have fancy letters? Does it have a famous cartoon character on it? What makes you want to buy it? When I was a child, I liked Cracker Jacks because there was a prize in every box!

2. Using pencil, draw the package outline. Draw really big—fill up the whole paper. I drew a famous soda bottle.

3. Draw the label. First draw its shape. Then add the special letters. For example, Coca-Cola has famous red and white swirling script letters. (It is okay if your drawing does not look exactly like the package.)

4. Look for a logo. A logo is a symbol that represents a product. Often a logo is instantly recognizable. For example, McDonald's has the golden arches. Wonder Bread has colorful dots. Does your product have a logo on it? Draw it.

5. Go over your drawing with bold outlines using a non-water-soluble marker. (You need a permanent marker for this. One brand name is Sharpie.)

6. Copy it. Draw a few copies of your picture or use a photocopy machine.

7. Paint your pictures with watercolor paints. Like Warhol, change the colors. I made bright blue and red soda! Display all your pictures together.

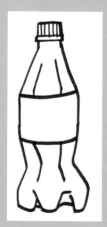 ▶  ▶

Supplies

Brand-name food product
Paper
Pencil
Non-water-soluble markers
Watercolor paint supplies

Famous ketchup.
—Matt, 10

I like soup.
—Danny, 10

Candy treats.—Sean, 10

My favorite cereal.—Amanda, 10

Try these, too!

Kitchen Collage

Pop artists Richard Hamilton and Tom Wesselman collected pictures of brand-name products and actual packages and pasted them into their artwork. Try it yourself! First, make a picture of a kitchen using paper shapes. Cut and paste shapes for a refrigerator, stove, table, sink, and cabinets. Now go shopping! Cut out little groceries from a supermarket circular, and paste them in your kitchen.

Create Your Own Brand

You know Nike, McDonald's, and Coca-Cola—why not create your own brand name? For example, what kind of soda can you invent? Think about who will buy your soda. What will be special about it? Design a bottle. Choose a fun name, and draw a label. You can also make up your own brand names for sneakers, clothing, or anything else. Draw your idea.

Pola-Cola.
—Sabatina, 8

Air Girl.—Michelle, 8

CARTOON IT!

ROY LICHTENSTEIN

The artist Roy Lichtenstein got his idea for this painting from a newspaper advertisement that showed a pretty girl holding a ball. She was advertising a hotel where people went on vacation in the Pocono Mountains in Pennsylvania. Lichtenstein didn't copy the ad exactly. He left out the words and painted the girl on a large canvas.

Lichtenstein turned the girl into a giant cartoon with bold outlines and flat bright colors. There are many strange things about her. Frozen in action, her hair blows in the wind and her arms reach up high. Her waist is so small, she looks like a doll. Look closely—her skin has tiny dots on it! Lichtenstein wanted to imitate Benday dots found in printed cartoons. Hold a magnifying glass up to a newspaper cartoon, and you will see dots that make the different shades of gray.

Lichtenstein was fascinated with the popular pictures we see around us every day and the stories that they tell. He copied hundreds of them in his famous cartoon style.

What is this girl doing? Where is she?

- How do you think she **feels**? What clues tell you that?
- How would you **describe** the way this girl looks? Look closely at her **face**. What do you notice about her **eyes** and her **mouth**? Why do you think her **mouth** is open?
- What is **unusual** about her **hair**? Why do you think it looks that way?

- What do you notice about her **skin**? Why do you think her skin looks that way?
- What is she doing with her **arms**? If she could move, what would **happen next**?
- What about this picture is like a **cartoon**? What about the girl looks **strange** or **make-believe**?

Girl with Ball, 1961
oil and synthetic polymer paint on canvas,
60¹⁄₄ x 36¹⁄₄ inches
The Museum of Modern Art, New York

Roy Lichtenstein got his idea for this painting from an advertisement of a girl with a ball. What do you think she was advertising or selling?

Bold outlines, funny faces, bright colors, and lots of dots!
This section invites you to paint your own Pop pictures in a colorful cartoon style.

Amazing Ads

Make art inspired by Lichtenstein

Paint a colorful cartoon of an advertisement. Add dot patterns!
When you watch television, what commercials do you see? When you look in a magazine, how many advertisements do you find? What do commercials and ads make you want to buy? Like Lichtenstein, copy an advertisement in your own creative way.

1. Find an advertisement in a magazine or newspaper. What is the picture selling? What makes the product look exciting? I found a cute picture of a dog kissing a lady. It is advertising perfume.

2. Copy it! Draw people from your advertisement in a cartoon style using pencil. Don't copy the picture exactly, just use it to get ideas for your artwork. Draw it on a large sheet of paper so you can paint it. (Draw lightly so you can erase.)

3. Exaggerate the features! I made a huge smile for the girl. Her head is really big. Look at the dog's fluffy tail and wide-open eye.

4. Go over your drawing with bold outlines using a non-water-soluble marker.

5. Print out dots. Cut out a piece of bubble wrap. Use a brush to wipe paint over the bubble wrap's dot pattern. Then turn the wrap over and gently press the painted bubble wrap onto your painting. Lift it up. Surprise! Notice all the dots.

6. Paint more dots with the eraser of a pencil. Dip the end of a pencil eraser into paint. Carefully press the eraser onto your paper to create dot patterns.

7. Paint bright, bold colors. To get a cartoon look, try not to mix all the colors together. See if you can paint within the lines. After your painting dries, you can go back over the outlines and add details with marker.

 ▶  ▶  ▶

Supplies

Paper	Non-water-soluble markers
Paint supplies	Bubble wrap
Advertisement to copy	Pencils with erasers

> Cartoons are really meant for communication. You can use the same forms, almost, for a work of art.—Roy Lichtenstein

Buy me dog treats!—Kelly, 9

Makeup girl.—Elizabeth, 11

Girl's world.—Lauren, 10

Try this, too!

Buy This!

Lichtenstein noticed the products we see in advertisements and all the things we buy. In giant cartoon pictures, he painted popular everyday things—school notebooks, sneakers, socks, refrigerators, washing machines, and more. What do you like to buy? Make a poster of a popular product such as your favorite sneakers, toy, doll, or anything else. Draw it large with thick outlines. Paint it with bright colors, and add dots. Write a slogan or words if you like.

I love electronic games.—Victoria, 10

Cartoon Rubbings

Draw a cartoon character or comic strip.
Then add dots and textures with crayon rubbings.

Donald Duck, Mickey Mouse, Bazooka Joe, and more. Lichtenstein copied all kinds of popular cartoons for his art. Sometimes, to imitate the look of printed Benday dots, he rubbed the side of a pencil on his paper against a piece of screening to get a dot pattern. Try it yourself!

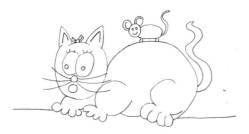

1. Find a favorite comic strip or cartoon character. You can also make up your own cartoon from your imagination.
2. Copy it! Draw it big so it fills up a large sheet of paper. You can draw one or more cartoon panels for your artwork. (Sketch it with pencil. It does not have to look exactly like the original cartoon.)
3. Add words. You can make a bubble that tells what the cartoon character is thinking or saying. Or write words in a box on the side that tells about the action in the cartoon.
4. *Swoosh! Zoom! Bang! Wham!* You can add words that tell about the sound or movement in your cartoon.
5. Outline your cartoon in marker.
6. Add dots with crayon rubbings. Ask an adult to help you find a scrap piece of window screening or another material with a raised dot pattern. Place the screening under your paper. Rub the side of a crayon on your paper over the screening. Watch how dots appear! (For safety, do not rub against a screen that is installed in a window.) If you like, find other textured objects around your home for your rubbings. For example, I made stripes by rubbing over cardboard. You can make a wood-grain pattern by rubbing over a door.
7. Color it in with bright colors. Try to stay inside the lines.

Supplies

Cartoon to copy
Paper
Pencil
Markers
Window screening
Crayons
Assortment of textured materials

by Megan Elizabeth, 9

My favorite cartoon.—Zachary, 9

Super cake!—Nicholas, 9

Knock, knock, whooooo's there?
—Lily, 9

How does she look?—Alessandra, 10

Try this, too!

Blow It Up!

Lichtenstein made huge paintings of cartoons that he copied from small printed comics. Sometimes he blew up the comic strips using a projector. Find a favorite cartoon such as Snoopy or SpongeBob. In school, use an opaque or overhead projector to enlarge the image—just trace the cartoon onto your paper. You can also use the enlarge setting on a photocopier, or art programs on a computer. Or just draw the cartoon really big on a large sheet of paper. Paint the picture in with bold colors and add dots. Then outline with a marker.

FAMOUS SYMBOLS

JASPER JOHNS

The artist Jasper Johns changed a map of the United States of America into a wild, wonderful work of art. Most maps have borders that are carefully drawn and neatly colored in. As you can see, this is not a real map. It is a painting of one that is all mixed up. Johns copied a map onto a large canvas. Then, painting quickly, he swooshed colorful paint in and around the states and let the paint smear and splatter. As he painted, he stenciled in the names of the states. Look closely . . . the colors are unusual. Blue usually stands for water, but in this picture it is painted all over the land!

Even though this map is really strange, you know it is the United States. How could you tell? Probably you have seen maps of this country so many times that you recognized it right away. Johns loved to change popular symbols into amazing abstract paintings. In addition to painting many maps, Johns painted flags, numbers, letters of the alphabet, and targets.

Can you name this country? How can you recognize it?

- Do you **live** in this country? If so, can you find the **state** where you live? Point out all the states that you have **visited**. Look closely. Are the names of the states in the right places?
- Can you find the **Atlantic Ocean** and the **Pacific Ocean**? Look at the colors of the oceans. What is unusual about them?
- Think of most maps you have seen. How is this one **different**? How many things can you find that are really **strange** about it?
- What is **unusual** about the way the artist used the color **blue** on this map?
- **Imagine** the artist **painting** this picture. How do you think he used his **brush**? What do you notice about the **paint**?

Art © Jasper Johns / Licensed by VAGA, New York, NY

- Notice all the **words**. How do you think he painted those?
- **Compare** the way this painting is made to *Girl with Ball* on page 17. How are they **different**? What, if anything, is **similar** about the two pictures?

Could you use a map like this one?

From mixed-up maps to fantastic flags, the art projects in this section invite you to turn popular symbols into creative works of art.

Mixed-Up Maps

Paint a colorful, crazy, mixed-up map of your country.

Most of the time, when we make a map, we draw the borders neatly and color inside the lines. Now, like Johns, instead of making a map that you can use, play with paint to make a funny map that is nothing like you have ever seen. Make an ocean red or land bright blue! See if people can tell what place it is when you are done.

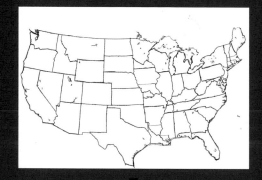

1. Find a map of your country. Then redraw it on a large sheet of paper—you do not have to copy it exactly. Sketch it in lightly. Or, make a large photocopy of a map (11 x 17 inches) on stiff paper. You can also print a map from the internet or buy one and paint right over it.

2. Paint it out. Don't color inside the lines! Like Johns, blend and smear gooey wet paint from one state or country into another. Let it drip and spatter. (Tip: As you paint, keep your colors clean—wash your brush each time you use a new color.)

3. Go wild with color and patterns. Instead of blue, I made yellow and orange water. I painted the states rainbow colors and used blue for land! Make fun designs. Paint in stripes, polka dots, or any other designs that you imagine. Let your paintbrush swirl around the map.

4. Add letters. Name the states, cities, countries, or oceans. Like Johns, you can paint with stencils or use letters. Or write them in with colored pencils or crayons after your painting dries. You can also add sticker letters.

5. Why not mix it up? You can turn your map upside down, draw it backward, put cities and states in the wrong places, or do anything else you can think up. Mix up the names of the states or make up new ones if you like. I wrote letters that have nothing to do with the real states. I call my picture *Alphabet America*.

Supplies

Map
Paper
Painting supplies
Alphabet stencils or stickers (optional)
Crayons or colored pencils

Take an object. Do something to it. Do something else to it.
—Jasper Johns

Colorful USA.—Michael J., 8

Snow America.—Angela, 10

Mixed-up states.—Sierra, 8

Paint across the country.—Kyle, 10

Try this, too!

Alphabet Play

A, B, C! Letters stand for sounds and become words that you can write. Picture a painting that's made of letters that don't spell anything at all. That's what Johns did in some of his paintings. He stenciled letters to create patterns and designs. Try it yourself. Using stencils or painting freehand, make a picture that is filled with letters. Create patterns by repeating the same letter. Make fun designs out of letters, write upside down, or paint anything else you imagine.

Alphabet design.—P.J., 10

Fun Flags

Change the designs and colors of a flag using sponge painting.
One night Johns had a dream that he painted a picture of an American flag. Later he actually began painting all kinds of colorful flags. Sometimes he changed the flag's colors to make abstract pictures. Instead of red, white, and blue, the stars and stripes are green in one of his flag paintings! Like Johns, turn your country's flag into a creative work of art.

▼

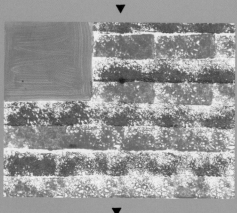

▼

1. Think about your country's flag. Where do you see it? What do the shapes and colors stand for? What is it a symbol for? My country is the United States of America.

2. Cut out shapes for your flag from clean sponges. (You can ask an adult to help.) I cut out stars. Then I made rectangles to stamp out the stripes. You can also cut out squares, circles, or other fun shapes. Or buy precut shapes, sponge brushes, and rollers from a craft store.

3. Get ready to paint. Pour each color of your paint onto a separate plastic plate. Dip a sponge into a color and press the sponge onto a piece of scrap paper. Practice stamping colors on your scrap sheet.

4. Color in the background. Color large areas of your picture by smearing paint. Wait a few minutes for the background to dry.

5. Stamp shapes for your flag. Change the colors. Instead of red and white, I stamped out pink and green stripes. I made bright pink stars on an orange background.

6. Play with the design. For example, for an American flag, why not make stripes that go up and down, instead of across? Or use a sponge brush to roll out curvy stripes. Stamp stars all over, or put them on the wrong side of the flag. Create new shapes! For instance, instead of stars, you can stamp out flowers or circles for states. Does your picture still remind you of the flag of your country?

Supplies

Sponges cut into shapes
Scissors

Sponge brushes or rollers
Paper
Paint supplies
Plastic plates

Colorful stars of America.—Jillian, 9

Wavy stripes.—Rachel, 8

Only one star!—Brendan, 8

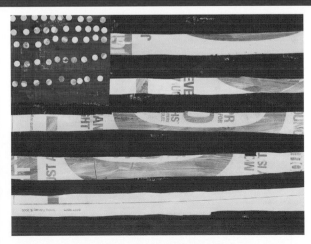

Green, white, and purple flag.—Angela, 9

Try this, too!

Colorful Collage Flags

To make his colorful flags, Johns first painted colors over sheets of newspaper. Then he cut and pasted pieces of the colored newspaper to form the stars and stripes of an American flag. Sometimes you can see through the paint and notice the newspaper's words and photos. Make your own collage flag. Paint pages of a newspaper different colors, and let them dry. Then cut out shapes from your painted newspaper, and glue them together to create your flag.

Dots and stripes!—Johnnel and Sarah, 10

R CYCLE Fu ART
ROBERT RAUSCHENBERG

The artist Robert Rauschenberg captured exciting moments in history in this picture. Look at the artwork—it is like a time capsule. The images show what was happening in the world around the time that Rauschenberg made his artwork in 1964. First he collected many photographs from magazines and newspapers. Then, using colorful ink, he copied them with a special way of printing called photo silkscreening.

The photograph in the center of this picture shows John F. Kennedy, the thirty-fifth president of the United States. Rauschenberg had first thought of using Kennedy's face in a picture after seeing Kennedy on television, and he made a sketch of him. He sent his drawing to Kennedy and later made many artworks of the popular president. Kennedy died just months before this one was created. President Kennedy set America moving in its adventures into outer space. Can you find an astronaut? What special things are going on in your world today?

What do you see in this picture? What is happening?

- The man in the center was **president** of the United States of America. Do you know his name? Who is the **leader** of your country today?
- What do you think the **man** is **doing**? What might he be **thinking** or **saying**? What is he doing with his **hand**?
- Find another **person**. What is he **doing**? **Where** do you think he is going?
- What else do you see in this picture?
- Play **a looking game**. How many things do you see that are **moving** or **floating**? How many things can you find that are **pointing**? What can you find that is **copied** more than once?

- Look at the **shapes**. How many things can you find that are **circle** shapes? Can you find **rectangles**? What other shapes do you see?
- How do you think this artwork was **made**? Where do you think the artist may have found these **photographs**?
- This picture features a **famous news event**. Look at the artwork. Can you guess what news is shown? (Hint: Where did people travel for the first time?)

Art © Robert Rauschenberg / Licensed by VAGA, New York, NY

Retroactive I, 1963
oil and silkscreen ink on canvas, 84 x 60 inches
Wadsworth Atheneum, Hartford, Connecticut

What is happening in your world today?
What important events will people remember?

Collect it! Clip it! Like Rauschenberg, find newspaper photos, junk, and other fun stuff in your surroundings that you can recycle for art.

Time Capsule Collage

Make art inspired by Rauschenberg

Make a collage of magazine and newspaper photos that show what is happening in your world. Then draw and paint on it!
The World Series, hurricanes, Harry Potter, electronic games . . . what's new? Think about all the people and things you see on television, in the news, in magazines, and in movies. Like Rauschenberg, collect photos that show what is exciting today. Imagine if people found your collection one hundred years in the future. What would they discover about your world?

1. What's new? Choose a subject for your collage. Here are some ideas: sports events, news stories, famous people, the latest technology, transportation today, cool fashion, kids' favorite things.
2. Clip pictures from magazines and newspapers. My artwork is about sports in the news, so I found photographs of athletes. Then I added pictures of things that move fast, such as a car and an airplane. Collect other printed materials such as stickers, wrapping paper, cards, ticket stubs, maps, menus, or anything else.
3. Arrange your materials on a large piece of paper or cardboard. Put pictures upside down or sideways. Move them around as you work. Then, when you're happy with the way they look, glue them down. (Tip: You might want to leave some empty spaces for your drawings and paint.)
4. Transfer it! Trace magazine pictures using pencil and tracing paper. Then flip the tracing paper over and lay it flat on your collage. Hold the tracing paper in place. Rub the back of the tracing paper with the side of a pencil, then lift it up. Surprise! Your drawing will appear on your collage.
5. Layer it! You can also paste or tape tracing paper to your collage to get exciting see-through pictures.
6. Paint it! Like Rauschenberg, brush on colorful paint. You can paint over and around your photographs and collage materials. *Splash!*

Supplies

Paper
Scissors
Glue
Paint supplies
Magazine pictures
Tracing paper
Pencil

Today's winners! —Marina, 9

Pretty and popular. —Sheila, 8

Exciting games. —Tatiana, 9

Try this, too!

Who Is My Hero?

Like Rauschenberg, make a print of someone who is a hero to you. Who do you admire? For example, you can show the president, a popular athlete, or your mother. First, make a simple collage about the person by gluing magazine pictures that remind you of him or her. Then print a face right over your collage. (Use Styrofoam printmaking—see page 10 for instructions.)

My favorite rap singer. —Melissa, 9

T. ash to Treasu. es

Make an artwork about the place you live by collecting things from your surroundings.

Rauschenberg lived in New York City. He walked around collecting things that he could use for use art. So many things are thrown away every day. Why not recycle some of them for art? An old tire, stuffed animals, magazines, broken doors! Rauschenberg attached these things to his artworks and brushed paint around them. Like Rauschenberg, collect stuff for your project that captures the place where you live.

▼

1. Look around! Collect things in your house or outside that you can use for your artwork. Look for things that will tell about the place where you live. I went on a beach walk, and I found toys, rope, shells, and bottle caps that washed up on the shore. Ask an adult to help you.

2. Find or buy a large sheet of sturdy cardboard or wood for your artwork.

3. Paint colors and designs that remind you of the place where you live. I painted bright blues, yellows, and oranges that remind me of sunshine and water at the beach. You can paint thick brushstrokes, and spatter paint. Let it dry.

4. Arrange your objects and materials on your painting. I pasted colorful bottle caps, sunglasses, goggles, rope, and other stuff in a swirling design. It reminds me of wind in a storm. Think about how your objects look together. Then glue them. If needed, ask an adult to help by using a hot-glue gun.

5. Attach things in other creative ways using wire, string, rope, or pipe cleaners. I hung a toy truck from rope. It swings back and forth!

6. Add finishing touches. Touch up some areas with paint. Or glue on more stuff. I added shells.

Supplies

Sheet of sturdy cardboard or wood
Collection of objects
Heavy glue or hot-glue gun
Scissors
Paint supplies
Wire, string, or rope to attach objects

Mall madness.—Erika and Jade, 10

Recycle America.—T.J.,
Lucas, Matt, and Taylor, 10

Try this, too!

Creative Combines

Rauschenberg once found a stuffed goat, put a tire around it, and painted its nose! He called his artworks "combines" because they were made of unusual combinations of objects, pictures, and paint. Collect junk—old plastic toys, stuffed animals, broken jewelry, or anything else. Glue the objects together in funny ways to make a sculpture. You can also glue your collection inside a box and add paint. (Ask an adult to use a hot-glue gun.)

A picture is more like the real world when it's made out of the real world!
—Robert Rauschenberg

Dreams and hopes.
—Noël, Julie, and Melissa, 9

33

THINK BIG

CLAES OLDENBURG

Think big! Imagine if you woke up and everything in your world was gigantic. Picture ice-cream treats that are bigger than you or a huge hamburger that you can nap on. The artist Claes Oldenburg changed everyday things into fantastic works of art by making them into huge sculptures. Take a look! These four ice-cream pops might be as long as your arms—each is almost two feet long. The giant pops were sewn out of colorful fake fur and filled with stuffing.

Oldenburg didn't stop there. He turned all kinds of ordinary things—a fan, a hamburger, a telephone, and musical instruments—into gigantic wobbly soft sculptures. He also created a lipstick, a spoon, a toothbrush, and other popular objects that stand taller than buildings! Look around. What will you create for your art?

What popular food do you see?

- Can you guess what popular **brand name** this sculpture is titled after? (Hint: You might buy these treats from a truck that drives past your house.)
- The artist **changed** a familiar food into a **playful** work of art. How are these different from real **ice-cream pops**?
- Look at the **corners** of each object. What do you notice? Imagine taking a **bite** from each of these. What would they **taste** like?
- What **flavors** might these be? Make up your own **silly names** for each of them. (I call one Tiger Treat!)
- What **materials** do you think the artist used to make this **sculpture**? How do you think he made it?
- Think of most **sculptures** or statues you have seen. What is **unusual** or **different** about this one?

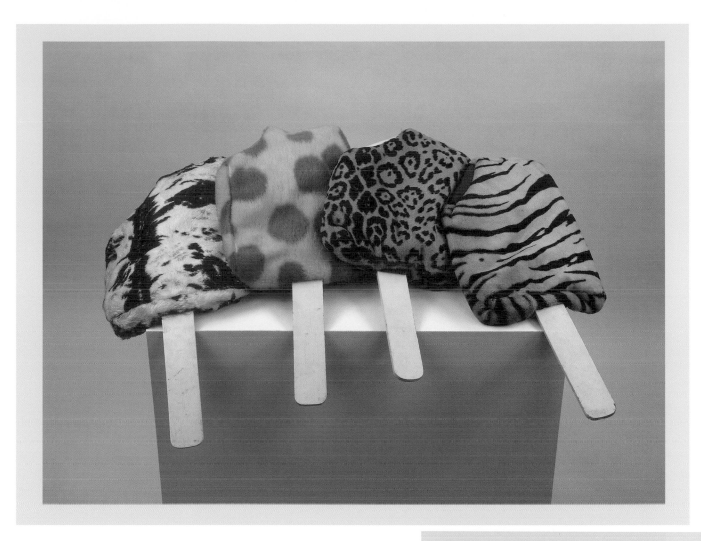

Soft Fur Good Humors, 1963
fake fur filled with kapok and wood painted with enamel
4 units, each 2 x 9½ x 19 inches
Private collection

• **Imagine** if you saw **giant** ice-cream pops like these in your home. What would you think? What would you do? Make up a **story** about how these pops became so **large**. What will **happen next**?

Pops, sundaes, cones, and shakes! What is your favorite ice-cream treat?

Ice cream, pizza, cell phones, and more. This section invites you to turn popular things and favorite foods into whimsical sculptures.

Soft Sculpture

Make art inspired by Oldenburg

Turn a popular food or object into a giant soft sculpture using felt or fabric.

Imagine a giant phone that is soft and cuddly or a pizza pillow that you can hug. Change something that normally feels hard into a plush cushioned artwork. Like Oldenburg, make a soft sculpture of one of your favorite things. You can use it as a pillow or a toy.

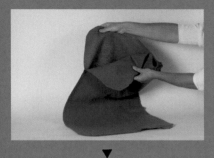

1. Choose an everyday object or food for your project such as a cell phone, a slice of pizza, a burger, or anything else. I made a giant laptop computer. (Tip: Choose something that has a simple shape so it will be easy to make.)

2. Cut a large shape for your object out of two pieces of felt. I cut out two rectangles for my computer. You can cut circles for a hamburger and buns. Cut large triangles for pizza.

3. Form a pillow. Squeeze a line of glue around the inside edge of the felt shape. (Leave one edge open so you can stuff it!) Glue the second felt shape to it. Or stitch the shapes together.

4. Cut and glue felt shapes for details. For my laptop computer, I added a lime green screen and colorful keys.

5. Add decorations. I glued beads, plastic flowers, and lace. I drew letters and numbers with glitter glue. (If needed, ask an adult to attach things with a hot-glue gun.)

6. Fill it with fabric scraps or stuffing from a craft store. Then close your sculpture by gluing or sewing the open ends together.

7. Add finishing touches. I attached a computer mouse and plug. I put a cute animal on my computer screen.

Supplies

Felt or plush fabric
Stuffing or fabric scraps
Scissors
Decorative materials such as yarn, sequins, or buttons
Hot-glue gun or heavy glue
Needle and thread optional

I make my work out of my everyday experiences which I find as perplexing and extraordinary as can be. —Claes Oldenburg

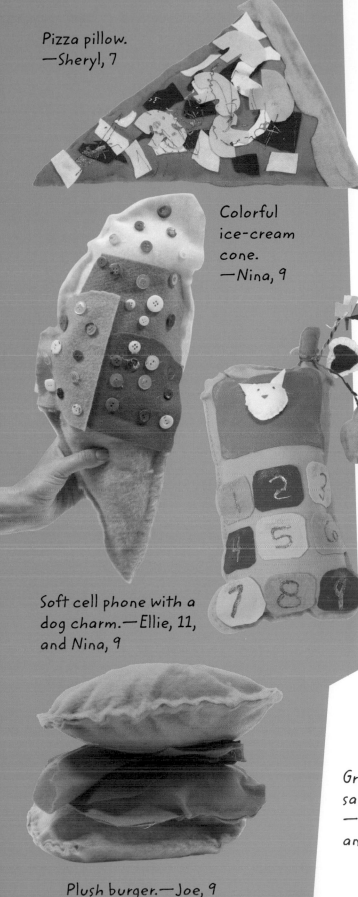

Pizza pillow.
—Sheryl, 7

Colorful ice-cream cone.
—Nina, 9

Soft cell phone with a dog charm.—Ellie, 11, and Nina, 9

Plush burger.—Joe, 9

Sculpture Paper Cutouts

Make a soft sculpture out of paper. Draw a large outline of your object or food on a large sheet of paper. Then, holding two papers back to back, cut out the shape from both sheets. Staple the edges together, but leave one end open. Stuff the sculpture with crumpled newspaper, and staple it shut. Then paint it. Look at the giant hot dog! We squirted yellow paint for mustard. Yummm!

Giant hot dog and fries!
—Project Most kids

Soft Sandwiches

Oldenburg once made a giant soft sandwich. He called it *BLT (Bacon, Lettuce, and Tomato Sandwich)*. Make a fake sandwich out of soft materials you find around your home. Collect clean sponges, felt, cotton balls, or yarn. Use sponges for bread, and cut out felt for cold cuts. Yellow yarn might be mustard and green fabric can be lettuce! What will you put on your sandwich?

Green sponge sandwich!
—Michael and Trippie, 9

Make It Big

Make a huge sculpture of an everyday object or food using papier-mâché and paint.

Picture a baseball bat that's as tall as a building or a giant toothbrush that reaches the sky! Working together, Oldenburg and his wife, Coosje van Bruggen, turned ordinary objects such as a hat, a spoon, a flashlight, and a button into gigantic outdoor sculptures. Try it yourself! Change a small thing into a huge work of art.

▼

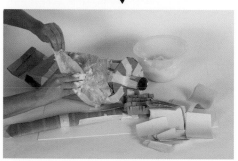

▼

1. Look around. Choose an object for your project. Pick something that will be easy to build. Here are some ideas: a pencil, crayons, a candy bar, a hamburger, a lollipop. I made a toothbrush and toothpaste.

2. Gather materials such as corrugated cardboard, tag board, cardboard boxes, paper towel rolls, brown paper bags, tinfoil, or newspaper that you can use to build your object. Ask an adult to help.

3. Construct a gigantic object. Cut and bend cardboard and other materials into shapes for your object. Tape the pieces together. To make a tube of toothpaste, I stuffed a paper bag with newspaper and added a cardboard roll. You can make a candy bar out of a cardboard box. Make a pencil or crayons out of cardboard tubes.

4. Wrap it with papier-mâché. Cut paper strips (about two inches wide) before you begin. Cover the table with wax paper so the papier-mâché won't stick to it. Prepare papier-mâché according to the package directions. Dunk a strip into the papier-mâché. Squeeze off excess. Piece by piece, wrap the entire sculpture with strips. Then give it a second layer.

5. Let it dry overnight, then paint it. Add details such as letters with a small brush or marker. I made up my own brand, *Super Toothpaste!* I added cotton for toothpaste.

Supplies

Materials to construct:
    poster board,
    cardboard,
    paper towel rolls,
    etc.
Paper strips

Tape
Papier-mâché paste: flour
    paste or Pritt (sold at
    craft stores)
Water
Scissors
Paint supplies
Markers

Wacky crayons.
—Ms. Reboli's art class

World's biggest candy bar.
—Project Most kids

A pencil that's bigger than you!—Project Most kids

Try these, too!

Triple decker.
—Project Most kids

Ice-Cream Dream

Make a giant ice-cream treat using papier-mâché. Create the scoops by blowing up balloons. Or crumple lots of newspaper into big round balls. (Use tape to keep the balls together.) Make a cone out of cardboard. Wrap them with papier-mâché. Paint your favorite flavors, and add sprinkles with glitter or beads. Squirt fake syrup by dripping colorful paint!

Really big banana split!
—Ms. Reboli's art class

Land of the Giants

To get ideas for his giant sculptures, Oldenburg made magazine collages and drawings. Find a magazine picture of an outdoor place such as a forest, ocean, or city. Then use magazine pictures to paste in gigantic things. For example, you might paste a huge burger in front of the royal palace!

Fast Food Fakes

by Matthew, 11

Sculpt your favorite fast food out of clay and paint it.
For his art, Oldenburg created a store and filled it with funny-looking fake food made out of plaster and paint. Sometimes he acted out shows in his store and sold his imitation food. Make your own fake-food feast by molding hamburgers, fries, pizza, hot dogs, and anything else you imagine out of clay.

1. What kind of fast food do you like? Hamburgers, hot dogs, pizza, tacos, Chinese food, or sushi to go? Choose a food for your project.

2. Squish the clay, and mold it into shapes for your food. Work on wax paper or cardboard so the clay does not stick to the table. I patted clay to make a hamburger and buns. I used a fork to scrape into the burger to get the look of meat. Roll clay between your hands for hot dogs. Use a plastic knife to slice French fries. Pat the clay flat and cut a round shape for a pizza pie.

3. Add details. I made a round tomato. Then I ripped up clay pieces for lettuce. You can also stick materials into your clay. I added beads to the bun for sesame seeds.

4. Let it air-dry overnight, then paint it. For a fun finishing touch, you can squirt red or yellow paint for ketchup or mustard.

5. Collect fast-food containers and other items for your project. Ask at a fast-food restaurant or look around your home. I added a French fry packet, a plastic fork, a plate, and a napkin.

6. Play store with friends, and pretend to sell your food! Make up a name for your fast-food company and add it to your project. I call mine *Fun Fries.*

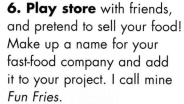

Supplies

Self-hardening clay
Clay tools or plastic knife
Paint supplies
Fast-food containers, disposable utensils, or other items
Decorative materials such as beads (optional)

We love hot dogs and hamburgers!—Nicholas, Michael, Karol, and Allison, 11

Two tacos. Yummm! —Megan and Travis, 11

Japanese sushi to go. —Ellen and Audrey, 11

Try this, too!

Make Room for Dessert

Oldenburg sculpted all kinds of fake desserts and displayed them in a pastry case. Pies, doughnuts, cookies, ice cream—what is your favorite treat? Make it out of clay. For example, mold a clay cupcake and decorate it with beads and plastic flowers. When it dries, paint it. Put it on a pretty paper plate or in a cupcake tin. Pretend you own a bakery or ice-cream shop, and sell your treats with play money.

Don't these look real?—Janet, Alexandra, and Allison, 11

REAL OR IMAGINARY?

GEORGE SEGAL

The artist George Segal captured people doing ordinary things in their daily lives. In his artworks, you might see people riding a bus, eating in a restaurant, or working at their jobs. In this sculpture, a man stops for a bite to eat at a diner. The woman behind the counter is serving coffee. The ghostly white people seem to be frozen in time.

Segal created these figures using an exciting way of making art called plaster casting. First he asked his friends to pose for him. Then he soaked bandages in wet plaster. Piece by piece, he placed the bandages on his models. When the plaster bandages hardened, he carefully lifted them off. He cast the models' legs, arms, feet, hands, body, and heads, and then put all the parts together to form life-sized people! Finally, for this artwork, he put his plaster people at a diner counter and added a real sugar container, lights, sink, and coffee makers. A Pop artist, Segal turned everyday people and everyday things into mysterious artworks.

What place is this? How can you tell?

- Notice the man who is **sitting**. What is he **doing** there? What might he be **thinking** or **feeling**?
- Look at the person who is **standing**. **Who** is she? What is she **doing**? What is she **holding** in her hand?
- How would you **describe** these people? How do they look? How do you think they **feel**?
- What is **strange** about this place? Why do you suppose there are no other seats around the man? What else is unusual?

- How would you describe the **mood** or feeling in this place? What gives you that idea?
- Have you ever been to a **place** like this? How is this scene **different** than it would be in real life? What about it is **similar**?
- Which parts of this artwork do you think the **artist made**? Which parts do you think the **artist bought** or **found**?
- Would you want to be in this **scene**? Why or why not? What would it be like?
- Make up a **story** about these **strange people** in this place.

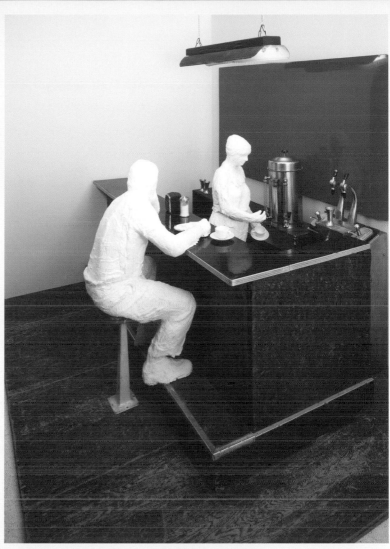

Art © The George and Helen Segal Foundation / Licensed by VAGA, New York, NY

The Diner, 1964–1966
plaster, wood, chrome, laminated plastic, Masonite, fluorescent lamp, glass, and paper
93³/₄ x 144¹/₄ x 96 inches
Walker Art Center, Minneapolis, Minnesota

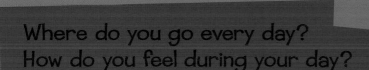

Where do you go every day? How do you feel during your day?

Cast it! Like Segal, work with a friend to create amazing body casts. Then add real props to tell a story!

Cast It

Make art inspired by Segal

Cast your hand with plaster gauze. Then paint and decorate it.
Segal became famous for his mysterious plaster people that he placed in real settings. Like Segal, make a body cast. Work with a partner to cast your hand. First, your friend will wrap your hand. When that's done, switch and wrap your partner's hand. (Using this same technique, you can also cast your feet.)

▼

▼

▼

1. Cut the plaster gauze into small strips, about 1 inch x 2 inches. Cut smaller pieces for fingers.

2. Cover your hand with petroleum jelly. When you wrap it, the gauze will easily slip off and will not stick to your skin.

3. Pose your hand. What can you say with your hands? For example, make a fist, or a peace sign, or pretend you are holding something. Or lay your hand flat on a table. Then hold your hand still as your partner works.

4. Wrap it! Have your partner dunk a plaster gauze strip into warm water. Gently squeeze off excess water. Piece by piece, wrap *one side* of your hand with plaster gauze. Then do a second layer. *Do not wrap both sides or you will not be able to slide it off!*

5. Wait a few minutes for plaster gauze to harden, then gently remove it. Let the cast dry completely overnight.

6. Paint it. You can create skin colors or paint wild designs and colors. Or, like Segal, leave it white. (For pale skin colors, mix orange, white, and a touch of red. For dark or tan skin, mix brown with a touch of red and white.)

7. Add materials. Collect things from your home. Glue on fake nails. Decorate the hand with rings and bracelets. What is the hand holding? Add a comb, fake flowers, a ball, a pencil, a cup, or anything else.

Supplies

Plaster gauze (available at craft or surgical supply stores)
Petroleum jelly
Water
Scissors
Paint supplies
Glue
Found materials

Somehow it still strikes me that daily life is baffling, mysterious, and unfathomable.
—George Segal

Strange blue hand.
—Erika, 9

So rich!
—Jessica, 9

I like to draw.—Gabriel, 13

Flowers for you.
—Amber, 9

Try these, too!

Cast a Face

Use a mold of a face from a craft store. Cast it with plaster gauze, then paint it and decorate it. Add yarn, paper strips, or a wig for hair! Glue on buttons for eyes and paper eyelashes.

Look into
my eyes.
—Melissa
and Julie, 10

Cast into Painting

The artist Jasper Johns made casts of body parts, such as faces, ears, and fingers, and attached them to some of his paintings. He also added real things such as brooms, paintbrushes, cups, and cans. Try it yourself! Attach a body cast and all kinds of objects to a picture.

Power of money.
—Miles, 9

Andy Warhol
American, 1928–1987

Andy Warhol grew up poor in a small town in Pennsylvania. His parents had moved to America from Czechoslovakia, and his father worked in a coal mine. As a teenager, Warhol earned money decorating store windows. He went to college to study commercial art in Pittsburgh, Pennsylvania. Later, he moved to New York City, where he lived with his mother and many cats—all named Hester. He created advertisements and illustrations for fashion magazines and made a lot of money.

During the 1960s, Warhol helped to create a new kind of art called Pop Art. He painted popular brand-name products such as Coca-Cola, Heinz ketchup, and Campbell's Soup in big, bold artworks. He also copied pictures of famous people and cartoons such as Popeye onto large paintings. Warhol invented a new way of making pictures. He collected photographs of celebrities and events from newspapers and magazines. Then he printed them out with bright colors. Instead of making art alone, Warhol hired creative people to work for him and help create prints. He called his art studio the Factory.

Warhol also made unusual movies. Once he made a film of himself sleeping! He also started his own magazine, *Interview*. He collected art, antiques, and thousands of everyday things. Warhol lived the American Dream—born into poverty, he became a famous artist and millionaire.

Roy Lichtenstein
American, 1923–1997

Roy Lichtenstein was born and raised in New York City, where he had a happy childhood. As a teenager, he painted as a hobby. During the summer, he studied art at the Art Students League, and later he went to college to study art at Ohio State University in Columbus. From 1943–1945, Lichtenstein served in the army during World War II. After the war, he returned to Ohio State to finish his education, and he got a job teaching there. In 1949, he married, and soon he had moved to Cleveland, Ohio, and had two sons. He sold his paintings and taught art. Later he decided to devote himself to painting.

In 1961, Lichtenstein began painting Pop Art pictures. For fun with his children, he painted large pictures of Bazooka Joe cartoons. He continued copying popular comics onto large paintings and became famous for it. His cartoon people were painted with bold outlines and bright colors. He added dots to imitate cartoons printed with Benday dots in newspapers.

Lichtenstein also painted huge cartoon pictures of everyday things such as washing machines, refrigerators, socks, sneakers, and notebooks. He copied famous paintings and created abstract designs, imaginary landscapes, and rooms, all in his cartoon style. He also made prints, sculptures, and murals. In 1970, Lichtenstein moved to Southampton, Long Island, in New York State, where he lived for many years.

Jasper Johns
American, born 1930

Jasper Johns was born in Augusta, Georgia. After his parents divorced, he was raised by aunts, uncles, and grandparents in South Carolina. Johns went to college at the University of South Carolina for one year. In 1949, he moved to New York City to study commercial art. But he was drafted into the army and went to Japan. Later he returned to New York and worked in a bookshop and designed window displays. Johns taught himself about art by studying the work of other artists. He lived in the same building as Robert Rauschenberg, and they became friends. They helped to create a new kind of art called Pop Art. During the 1950s, Johns began exhibiting his work, and he quickly became successful.

Johns became famous for his unusual paintings of maps, flags, letters, numbers, and targets. Picture an American flag with gray stars and stripes or a map of the United States that's filled with messy paint. Sometimes he attached objects to his paintings, such as brooms, paintbrushes, cups, and cans. He also sculpted casts of body parts and attached them to his pictures. Johns also made prints, drawings, and sculptures. He worked with the famous composer John Cage and designed costumes for the Merce Cunningham dance company. In the 1980s, Johns moved to the island of St. Martin.

Robert Rauschenberg
American, born 1925

Robert Rauschenberg was born in Port Arthur, Texas, an oil refinery town. He had dyslexia, a learning disability that made it difficult for him to read. He went to college to study pharmacy, and later he was drafted into the navy. During a break, he visited a museum and for the first time he saw famous paintings. He started drawing and later studied at the Kansas City Art Institute and School of Design. He traveled to Paris to study art, where he met his future wife.

In 1949, he settled in New York City. He moved into a building where the artist Jasper Johns lived, and they became friends. They designed store windows to earn a living. At times, Rauschenberg was so poor that he only had twenty-five cents a day to buy bread, peanut butter, and milk. He walked around collecting throwaway junk that he used in his artworks. He also collected thousands of photos and printed them onto huge pictures and added colorful paint. Rauschenberg sold his art and eventually became a millionaire. Sometimes he even gave people presents on *his* birthday!

Rauschenberg also invented artworks that move and make sounds. For fifteen years, he worked with the Merce Cunningham Dance Company designing sets and costumes, and later he became a lighting director and stage manager. He was also a performer. In 1971, he moved to Florida, where he lives today.

Claes Oldenburg
American, born 1929

Claes Oldenburg was born in Sweden. When he was a baby, his family moved to America, and they eventually settled in Chicago. As a young man, Oldenburg studied art at Yale University in Connecticut. After he graduated, he returned to Chicago and worked as a reporter. In 1956, Oldenburg moved to New York City, where he made friends with many artists. For his art, Oldenburg created actual places that you could walk into. He acted out unusual performances in them, called Happenings. During the 1960s, he rented a store and filled it with fake food and other things that he had sculpted. In The Store, he put on shows and sold his art goods.

In 1962, Oldenburg began making gigantic soft sculptures of everyday objects. He created soft fans, maps, musical instruments, food, and more, all sewn from fabric or vinyl and stuffed. Later he began sketching ideas for huge sculptures that could be built outside. In 1969, his first outdoor sculpture was constructed— a gigantic lipstick that was taller than a building! In 1976, Oldenburg began working with the writer Coosje van Bruggen, and a year later they married. Together they have created more than forty sculptures of huge objects in the United States and Europe. On a city street, for example, you might see a gigantic baseball bat that reaches the sky! Oldenburg and his wife continue making art together today.

George Segal
American, 1924–2000

George Segal was born in the Bronx, part of New York City. When he was a teenager, his family moved to a farm in New Jersey. Segal helped on the farm while he studied art and art education in college. As a young man, Segal married and bought his own chicken farm. A few years later, he took up painting again and got a job teaching art. He began selling his artworks and eventually became famous.

In 1958, Segal changed his chicken coops into art studios. He built sculptures of people out of materials he had on the farm, such as chicken wire, burlap, and plaster. In 1961, he started making body casts of people using plaster bandages. He placed his white-plaster people in settings filled with real objects— furniture, windows, cups, or even a real subway car! He captured scenes of daily life such as riding on a bus or eating in a restaurant.

In the 1970s, he began pouring plaster into the body casts, using them as molds. He painted his plaster people in bold colors to show their moods. He also created bronze figures and put them in outdoor settings. Some of his later works told about events in history. Today Segal's sculptures are in museums all over the world.

About the Author

Joyce Raimondo, creator of the Art Explorers series, is director of Imagine That! Art Education, specializing in helping children access the arts. As a visiting author to schools and a consultant, she teaches children how to look at famous artworks and use art history as a springboard for their own creativity. Her clients include the Pollock-Krasner House and Study Center, Children's Television Workshop, and numerous museums.

She is the author of The Museum of Modern Art's acclaimed Art Safari series of children's books, kits, and online program. From 1992–2000, she served as family programs coordinator at MoMA in New York, where she created programs that teach children and adults how to enjoy art.

A painter and sculptor, Joyce Raimondo has contributed illustrations to the *New York Times* and the *Boston Globe,* and she has appeared on *Blue's Clues, Fox Breakfast Time,* and *NBC News.* She divides her time between Manhattan and East Hampton, New York. Visit her on the web at www.joyceraimondo.com.

Author photo by Kathleen Bilfulco

Joyce and Buddy

Acknowledgments

As director of Imagine That! Art Education, I implement workshops designed to teach children how to enjoy art history. I ask students to describe what they see in famous artworks and follow up with their own creations. Much of the children's art featured in this book was made during these workshops. A special thanks to the children who contributed artwork. They are listed next to their wonderful creations.

Gratitude is given to my editors, Julie Mazur and Laaren Brown, for bringing clarity to the development of the fourth volume in the Art Explorers series. I am also thankful to Ed Miller, the designer, who created the book's lively graphics, and to Frank Roccanova and Kathleen Bilfulco for their photographic contributions.

Grateful acknowledgment is due to the schools who participated in this project: Chestnut Hill, Daniel Street, Northside, Project Most, Roanoke Avenue, Ross, Southampton, Springs, and Woodward Parkway. Special thanks is given to those who arranged the programs: Mary Jane Aceri, Tim Bryden, Sue Cardillo, Cathleen Goebel, Kelly Hren, Robin Laban, Rebecca Morgan, and Debbie Silverblank, and to the art teachers whose students produced works for this book: Ricki Weisfelner, Cara Palermo, Allyssa Gilman, Lois Reboli, and Melissa Haupt. Appreciation is given to the Nassau and Suffolk Boards of Cooperative Education, which funded many of these workshops.

Together, let's keep art in the schools!

by Allison, Alexandra, Janet, Danielle, Rebecca, Matthew, Stephanie, and Cathleen, 11